SUCCESS COMES

WHEN

YOU DISCONECT

FROM

NEGATIVE

PEOPLE

Major Prophet PD John
P.O. BOX 4016
Mwanza - Tanzania
Phone number:
+255 762 415 790/ +255 759 204 744
Yohanayona3@gmail.com
www.hlcentre.info

ISBN : 9798328211901
First edition ©2024.
Imprint: Independently published

Chief Editor:
Josia pd John
josiajohn735@gmail.com
Dar es salaam - Tanzania
Tel: +255 758588127/ +255 693522834

I

Success Comes When You Disconnect from Negative People

Dedication:

To all those who have the courage to disconnect from negativity and embrace success with open arms,

This book is dedicated to you. May you find the strength and determination to remove toxic influences from your life and thrive in a positive and empowering environment. Remember, success comes when you choose to surround yourself with positivity and rise above the negativity that holds you back.

Prophet Dr PD John

Preface:

In today's fast-paced and interconnected world, achieving success is a goal that many of us strive for. Whether it's personal fulfillment, career advancement, or financial prosperity, success holds a different meaning for each individual. We invest significant time, effort, and resources into improving ourselves, acquiring new skills, and setting ambitious goals. However, there is a critical factor that often goes unnoticed or underestimated—the influence of the people we surround ourselves with.

This book, *"Success Comes When You Disconnect from Negative People,"* explores the profound impact negative individuals can have on our lives and the importance of disconnecting from them in our pursuit of success. It delves into the psychological, emotional, and social aspects of how negative people can hinder our progress and outlines strategies to build healthier, more positive relationships that nurture our growth.

The journey to success is rarely a solitary one. We rely on the support, guidance, and encouragement of those around us. But what happens when the people we depend on become a source of negativity? When their pessimism, criticism, and toxic behavior drain our energy, erode our self-esteem, and hinder our progress? It is in these moments that we need to recognize the profound impact negative people have on our lives and make the courageous decision to disconnect from them.

In the following chapters, we will explore the characteristics and behaviors of negative people, helping you identify and understand their influence on your well-being. We will delve into the psychological dynamics at play, examining how negativity affects our self-esteem, confidence, and belief in our abilities. Armed with this knowledge, we will embark on a journey of self-reflection to evaluate our social circle and determine who supports our success and who holds us back.

Disconnecting from negative people is not an easy task. It requires courage, resilience, and determination. We will explore strategies to create healthy boundaries, assert ourselves in toxic relationships, and communicate our intentions to disconnect. We will also discuss the emotional challenges that may arise from severing ties with negative individuals, providing guidance on overcoming guilt and loneliness.

But disconnecting is only the first step. To truly achieve success, we need to cultivate a positive environment that fosters growth. We will discuss strategies for finding and nurturing relationships with like-minded, supportive individuals who will inspire and uplift us on our journey. Additionally, we will explore the power of mentorship and role models and the role they play in propelling us toward our goals.

Success is not just about external achievements; it starts with developing a success mindset. We will delve into the importance of cultivating a positive and growth-oriented mindset, overcoming self-doubt, and embracing failures as valuable learning experiences. Furthermore, we will provide practical tips for staying motivated, focused, and resilient in the face of challenges.

Lastly, we will address the significance of sustaining our success over the long term. Disconnecting from negative people is not a one-time event; it requires ongoing commitment and self-reflection. We will explore strategies for maintaining our disconnection, dealing with potential relapses, and building a support system of positive individuals who will cheer us on as we thrive.

As you embark on this transformative journey, remember that success is within your reach. By disconnecting from negative people, you are reclaiming control over your life and creating an environment that fosters your growth and success. This book aims to provide you with the tools, insights, and inspiration to make that crucial shift and embark on a path that leads to a more fulfilling and prosperous future.

May this book empower you to disconnect from negativity, embrace positivity, and embark on a remarkable journey toward the success you deserve.

Best wishes,

[Prophet PD John]

My Testimony

Throughout my journey as a young prophet in ministry, I have faced many challenges and obstacles that have tested my faith and perseverance. I have had to endure trials and tribulations that have pushed me to my limits, but through it all, I have learned valuable lessons and have grown stronger in my faith.

One of the biggest challenges I faced in my ministry was dealing with negative people. There were individuals who doubted my calling, criticized my methods, and tried to bring me down at every turn. These negative influences cast a shadow over my ministry and made it difficult for me to fully focus on my purpose.

I realized that in order to truly succeed in my ministry, I needed to disconnect from these negative people. So, I made the difficult decision to distance myself from those who were not supportive of my calling and who brought nothing but negativity into my life. It was not easy, and there were times when I felt lonely and isolated, but I knew that in order to move forward in my ministry, I needed to surround myself with positivity and encouragement.

As I began to disconnect from negative people, I noticed a shift in my ministry. I felt a renewed sense of purpose and passion for spreading the word of God, and I saw an increase in the number of people who were touched by my message. I was able to focus on my calling without the distractions of negativity, and I began to see success in my ministry like never before.

Through this experience, I learned that success truly does come when you disconnect from negative people. When you surround yourself with positivity and encouragement, you are able to fully embrace your calling and walk in the purpose that God has for you. It may not be easy to walk away from negative influences, but the rewards that come from doing so are well worth it.

In conclusion, as a young prophet in ministry, I have faced my fair share of challenges and obstacles. But through it all, I have learned that disconnecting from negative people is crucial to achieving success in my ministry. By surrounding myself with positivity and encouragement, I have been able to fully embrace my calling and walk in the purpose that God has for me. And for that, I am truly grateful.

Table of Contents:

Introduction:

In today's fast-paced and interconnected world, the pursuit of success has become a common goal for individuals across various domains of life. Whether it is personal fulfillment, career advancement, or financial prosperity, success holds a different meaning for each person. It is a reflection of our aspirations, dreams, and the desire to lead a fulfilling and purposeful life. But what factors contribute to our success, and what obstacles hinder our progress?

In this book, ***"Success Comes When You Disconnect from Negative People,"*** we will explore the profound impact that negative individuals can have on our lives and the crucial role of disconnecting from them in our journey towards success. We will delve into the meaning of success, the detrimental effects of negative people, and establish the thesis that disconnecting from negative individuals is essential for achieving true success.

Defining Success and Its Significance:

Before we delve into the importance of disconnecting from negative people, it is essential to define success and understand its significance in personal and professional growth. Success is not merely measured by external achievements or material possessions, but rather by the fulfillment and contentment we experience as individuals. It encompasses the realization of our goals, the development of our skills and talents, and the alignment of our actions with our values and purpose.

Scripture reminds us of the significance of true success:

1. **Joshua 1:8:** *"Keep this Book of the Law always on your lips; meditate on it day and night, so that you may be careful to do everything written in it. Then you will be prosperous and successful."* This verse emphasizes the connection between success

and living according to God's Word. True success flows from aligning our actions with His teachings, finding purpose in His plan, and seeking His guidance in all that we do.

2. **Proverbs 16:3:** *"Commit to the LORD whatever you do, and he will establish your plans."* Success involves committing our endeavors to God, recognizing that our achievements are not solely dependent on our efforts but on His divine guidance and intervention. By aligning our pursuits with His will, we open ourselves to the path of true success.

The Impact of Negative People:

Negative people can cast a dark shadow over our lives, hindering our personal and professional growth. Their pessimism, criticism, and toxic behavior can drain our energy, erode our self-esteem, and impede our progress towards success. It is important to recognize the profound impact that negative individuals can have on our overall well-being.

Scripture provides insights into the influence of negative people:

1. **Proverbs 22:24-25:** *"Do not make friends with a hot-tempered person, do not associate with one easily angered, or you may learn their ways and get yourself ensnared."* This verse warns us of the influence of negative individuals. Associating with them can lead us astray, adopting their destructive behaviors and attitudes. Disconnecting from negative people is a necessary step to protect ourselves from their detrimental influence.

2. *1 Corinthians 15:33:* *"Do not be misled: 'Bad company corrupts good character.'"* Our choice of company has a significant impact on our character and behavior. Negative individuals can gradually erode our values, aspirations, and success. Disconnecting from them is not a sign of weakness but a way to safeguard our character and preserve our journey towards success.

The Thesis: Disconnecting from Negative People is Crucial for Achieving Success:

Based on the definition of success and the understanding of the impact of negative people, we establish the thesis that disconnecting from negative individuals is a crucial step in achieving true success. By disconnecting, we create space in our lives for positive influences, nurture healthier relationships, and cultivate an environment that supports our growth and development.

Throughout this book, we will explore strategies for recognizing negative people, understanding the psychological impact of their presence, evaluating our social circle, and developing the resilience and mindset necessary to disconnect. We will also discuss the importance of cultivating positive relationships and creating a supportive environment that propels us towards success.

In conclusion, the journey to success is not solely determined by our individual efforts. It is greatly influenced by the people we surround ourselves with. Disconnecting from negative individuals is essential for creating a space that fosters growth, positive mindset, and resilience. In the following chapters, we will embark on a transformative exploration of the impact of negative people, the strategies for disconnecting, and the importance of cultivating positive relationships in our pursuit of true success.

May this book empower and inspire you to disconnect from negativity, embrace positive influences, and embark on a remarkable journey towards the success you deserve.

Best wishes on your path to success!

[Prophet PD John]

Chapter 1:

Recognizing Negative People

In our pursuit of success, it is crucial to be able to recognize the presence of negative people in our lives. These individuals can have a profound impact on our well-being, personal growth, and ultimately, our success. In this chapter, we will explore the characteristics and behaviors of negative people, differentiate between constructive criticism and negativity, identify toxic relationships, and examine real-life examples that illustrate the detrimental effects negative individuals can have on our journey towards success.

Characteristics and Behaviors of Negative People:

Negative people exhibit specific characteristics and behaviors that set them apart from those who are positive and supportive. By recognizing these traits, we can identify the negative influences in our lives and take appropriate action.

Scripture provides insights into the characteristics of negative people:

1. **Proverbs 22:24:** *"Do not make friends with a hot-tempered person, do not associate with one easily angered."* This verse warns against associating with individuals who have a hot temper. Negative people often display anger and irritability as part of their behavior, which can create a toxic and hostile environment.

2. **Proverbs 18:2:** *"Fools find no pleasure in understanding but delight in airing their own opinions."* Negative individuals tend to be self-centered and unwilling to understand others. They prioritize their own opinions and perspectives, dismissing those of others. This behavior can hinder open communication and collaboration.

Differentiating Between Constructive Criticism and Negativity:

While constructive criticism can be valuable for personal growth and improvement, negativity only brings us down. It is essential to distinguish between the two in order to filter out the harmful influence of negative people.

Scripture guides us in discerning between constructive criticism and negativity:

1. **Proverbs 27:6:** *"Wounds from a friend can be trusted, but an enemy multiplies kisses."* This verse highlights the importance of trusting the criticism and feedback that comes from genuine friends. Constructive criticism from a caring source is intended to help us grow and should be valued. On the other hand, negative people may offer insincere flattery to manipulate or deceive us.

2. ***Proverbs 12:18:*** *"The words of the reckless pierce like swords, but the tongue of the wise brings healing."* Negative individuals tend to be reckless with their words, using them as weapons to hurt and demean others. Constructive criticism, on the other hand, is delivered with wisdom and the intention to help, not harm.

Identifying Toxic Relationships and Their Effects on Success:

Toxic relationships, characterized by negativity, manipulation, and emotional abuse, can severely hinder our personal and professional success. It is crucial to recognize these relationships and their effects in order to protect ourselves and create a healthier environment.

Scripture warns against the dangers of toxic relationships:

1. **_Proverbs 13:20:_** _"Walk with the wise and become wise, for a companion of fools suffers harm."_ Associating with negative and foolish individuals can lead to harm. Toxic relationships drain our energy, lower our self-esteem, and impede our progress towards success.

2. **_Proverbs 25:26:_** _"Like a muddied spring or a polluted well are the righteous who give way to the wicked."_ Allowing toxic individuals into our lives can contaminate our own righteousness and purity. It is essential to recognize and address toxic relationships to protect our well-being and maintain a positive mindset.

Case Studies and Real-Life Examples:

To reinforce the impact of negative people on success, this chapter includes case studies and real-life examples that highlight the detrimental effects of negative influences on individuals' personal and professional lives. By examining these examples, readers can better understand the consequences of allowing negative people to remain in their lives and gain inspiration to take action.

In conclusion, recognizing negative people is the first step in protecting ourselves and creating an environment conducive to success. By understanding their characteristics and behaviors, differentiating between constructive criticism and negativity, and identifying toxic relationships, we gain the tools to eliminate negative influences from our lives. Real-life examples serve as reminders of the profound impact negative people can have on our journey towards success.

May this chapter equip you with the knowledge and discernment to recognize negative people and take the necessary steps to disconnect from their harmful influence.

Chapter 2:

Understanding the Psychological Impact

In Chapter 2, we will delve into the profound psychological impact that negative people can have on our journey towards success. By exploring psychological theories, examining the effects on self-esteem and confidence, and understanding how negativity breeds self-doubt and fear of failure, we will gain insights into the detrimental influence of negative individuals. Moreover, we will provide strategies for overcoming the psychological impact and reclaiming our confidence and resilience.

Psychological Theories Explaining the Influence of Negativity on Success:

To understand the psychological impact of negative people, we will explore various psychological theories that shed light on this phenomenon. These theories provide valuable insights into the mechanisms through which negativity affects our thoughts, emotions, and behavior.

Scripture provides wisdom regarding the power of our thoughts and mindset:

1. ***Romans 12:2:*** *"Do not conform to the pattern of this world but be transformed by the renewing of your mind."* This verse emphasizes the importance of renewing our minds and resisting the negative patterns of the world. It reminds us that our thoughts shape our beliefs, attitudes, and ultimately, our success. Disconnecting from negative people allows us to free our minds from their detrimental influence.

2. ***Philippians 4:8:*** *"Finally, brothers and sisters, whatever is true, whatever is noble, whatever is right, whatever is pure, whatever is lovely, whatever is admirable—if anything is excellent or praiseworthy—think about such things."* This verse

guides us to focus on positive and uplifting thoughts. By intentionally directing our thoughts towards positivity, we counteract the negative impact of others' pessimism and cultivate a success-oriented mindset.

How Negative People Affect Our Self-Esteem and Confidence:

Negative people can erode our self-esteem and confidence through constant criticism, belittlement, and comparison. Understanding how they impact our self-perception is crucial for reclaiming our self-worth.

Scripture reminds us of our inherent value and worth:

1. ***Psalm 139:14:*** *"I praise you because I am fearfully and wonderfully made; your works are wonderful, I know that full well."* This verse affirms our inherent worth as unique creations of

God. By recognizing our own worthiness, we become less susceptible to the negative opinions and judgments of others.

2. *Ephesians 2:10:* *"For we are God's handiwork, created in Christ Jesus to do good works, which God prepared in advance for us to do."* We are reminded that we are created for a purpose and equipped with unique abilities. Embracing this truth empowers us to rise above negative criticism and pursue our calling with confidence.

The Role of Negativity in Creating Self-Doubt and Fear of Failure:

Negative people can instill self-doubt and fear of failure within us, leading to a lack of confidence in our abilities and a reluctance to take risks. Understanding these dynamics is essential for breaking free from their grip.

Scripture provides encouragement in overcoming fear and doubt:

1. **2 Timothy 1:7:** *"For God has not given us a spirit of fear, but of power and of love and of a sound mind."* This verse reminds us that fear does not come from God. By embracing His power and love, we can overcome the fear instilled by negative individuals and move forward in confidence.

2. **Psalm 56:3:** *"When I am afraid, I put my trust in you."* Trusting in God allows us to overcome our fears and doubts. By relying on His strength and guidance, we can conquer the self-doubt created by negative people and step into our true potential.

Strategies for Overcoming the Psychological Impact of Negative People:

To reclaim our confidence and resilience, we need practical strategies to overcome the psychological impact of negative people. These strategies empower us to build a strong foundation for success.

Scripture offers guidance on resilience and mindset:

1. ***James 1:2-4:*** *"Consider it pure joy, my brothers and sisters, whenever you face trials of many kinds because you know that the testing of your faith produces perseverance. Let perseverance finish its work so that you may be mature and complete, not lacking anything."* This verse encourages us to find joy in adversity and see it as an opportunity for growth. By reframing our experiences with negative people as opportunities for personal development, we can cultivate resilience and emerge stronger.

2. ***Proverbs 3:5-6:*** *"Trust in the LORD with all your heart and lean not on your own understanding; in all your ways submit to him, and he will make your paths straight."* Trusting in God's guidance allows us to release our burdens and find direction. By surrendering our worries and

concerns about negative people to Him, we free ourselves from their psychological impact and open ourselves to His guidance towards success.

Personal Testimony:

I was once surrounded by negative people who constantly criticized and belittled me. Their words and behaviors chipped away at my self-esteem and confidence, leaving me filled with self-doubt and fear of failure. It was a challenging and draining time in my life, but I refused to let their negativity define me.

To overcome the psychological impact of negative people, I began by seeking support from positive individuals who believed in me. Their encouragement and affirmation helped counteract the damaging effects of the negative voices in my life. I also immersed myself in personal development resources, such as books and podcasts, that focused on building resilience and cultivating a positive mindset.

Prayer and meditation became essential practices in my journey. I sought guidance from a higher power and surrendered my worries and insecurities to God. This helped me regain my sense of purpose and find strength in knowing that I am fearfully and wonderfully made.

By implementing these strategies and surrounding myself with positive influences, I gradually reclaimed my confidence and silenced the self-doubt that had plagued me for so long. I embraced the truth that I am capable of achieving success and pursued my goals with renewed determination.

Today, I stand as a testament to the power of disconnecting from negative people and reclaiming control over my own mindset. I have achieved milestones I once thought were impossible, and I continue to grow and thrive on my journey towards success.

May my testimony inspire and encourage others to rise above the negativity in their lives and embrace the limitless possibilities that await them.

In conclusion, understanding the psychological impact of negative people is crucial for reclaiming our confidence, self-esteem, and resilience. By exploring psychological theories, recognizing the effects on self-doubt and fear of failure, and implementing strategies for overcoming these challenges, we can break free from the grip of negativity and pursue our path to success.

May this chapter empower you to recognize the psychological impact of negative people and equip you with the tools and insights to reclaim your confidence, nurture a positive mindset, and forge ahead on your journey towards success.

Chapter 3:

Evaluating Your Social Circle

In Chapter 3, we will explore the significance of evaluating our social circle and its impact on our success. By assessing the people in our lives, understanding the concept of social contagion, identifying positive and negative influences, and taking steps to disconnect from negative individuals while nurturing positive relationships, we can create a supportive network that fosters our growth and achievement.

Assessing the People in Your Social Circle and Their Influence on Your Success:

To evaluate our social circle, we must examine the individuals who surround us and assess the impact they have on our lives. By considering their attitudes, behaviors, and values, we can gain insight into their influence on our journey towards success.

Scripture provides guidance on the importance of choosing our companions wisely:

1. ***Proverbs 13:20:*** *"Walk with the wise and become wise, for a companion of fools suffers harm."* This verse emphasizes the wisdom of associating with wise individuals. Surrounding ourselves with those who uplift, inspire, and encourage us enables us to grow and achieve success. Conversely, negative influences can cause harm to our well-being and hinder our progress.

2. ***Proverbs 27:17:*** *"As iron sharpens iron, so one person sharpens another."* The people we surround ourselves with can either sharpen us or dull our edges. Positive and like-minded individuals have the potential to inspire and challenge us to become better versions of ourselves, while negative individuals can hinder our growth. Evaluating our social circle allows us to align ourselves with those who sharpen us on our journey to success.

The Concept of Social Contagion and Its Relation to Negative People:

Social contagion refers to the spread of attitudes, emotions, and behaviors within a social network. Understanding this concept is vital in recognizing how negative people can influence us and impact our success.

Scripture reminds us of the influence of those around us:

1. *1 Corinthians 15:33:* "*Do not be misled: 'Bad company corrupts good character.'*" This verse emphasizes the potential corrupting influence of negative people. Just as a contagious disease spreads, negative attitudes and behaviors can permeate our lives and hinder our character development and success. Evaluating our social circle allows us to protect ourselves from this contagion.

2. **Proverbs 22:24-25:** *"Do not make friends with a hot-tempered person, do not associate with one easily angered, or you may learn their ways and get yourself ensnared."* Associating with negative individuals can lead us down a destructive path. Their behaviors and attitudes can become a snare that entraps us in negativity. By evaluating our social circle, we can break free from these ensnaring influences.

Identifying the Positive and Negative Influences within Your Social Network:

To create a supportive and nurturing social circle, we must identify the positive and negative influences present in our lives. This process allows us to determine which relationships to prioritize and which ones may require distance or disconnection.

Scripture guides us in discerning positive and negative influences:

1. **Proverbs 27:6:** *"Wounds from a friend can be trusted, but an enemy multiplies kisses."* Positive influences are often those who offer genuine feedback, constructive criticism, and support. They may challenge us to grow, but their intentions are rooted in love and care. Negative influences, on the other hand, often display insincere flattery and selfish motives. Identifying and differentiating these influences allows us to foster healthier relationships.

2. **Proverbs 13:20:** *"Walk with the wise and become wise, for a companion of fools suffers harm."* Wise and positive influences contribute to our wisdom and growth. They inspire us to achieve our goals and uplift us in times of difficulty. Foolish and negative influences, however, can lead us astray and hinder our progress. Evaluating our social circle enables us to align ourselves with the wise and distance ourselves from the foolish.

Steps to Determine Who to Disconnect from and Who to Nurture in Your Social Circle:

Taking deliberate steps to disconnect from negative individuals while nurturing positive relationships is essential for creating a social circle that supports our success. By following a structured approach, we can make informed decisions about our social connections.

Scripture provides principles for discernment and guidance in relationships:

1. **Proverbs 3:5-6:** *"Trust in the LORD with all your heart and lean not on your own understanding; in all your ways submit to him, and he will make your paths straight."* Trusting in God's guidance allows us to navigate our relationships with wisdom and discernment. By seeking His guidance in evaluating our social circle, we can make choices that align with His plan for our lives.

2. ***Proverbs 16:3:*** *"Commit to the LORD whatever you do, and he will establish your plans."* Committing our decisions and relationships to God ensures that we are aligned with His will. By submitting our social circle to Him, we invite His wisdom and intervention in choosing who to disconnect from and who to nurture.

Personal Testimony:

In my own journey, evaluating my social circle was a transformative process. I took inventory of the people in my life and reflected on their influence on my well-being and success. Through prayer and discernment, I identified negative individuals who were draining my energy, undermining my confidence, and impeding my progress. It was not an easy decision, but I realized that their presence was hindering my growth.

Simultaneously, I recognized the positive influences in my life—those who believed in me, encouraged me, and challenged me to reach my full potential. I intentionally nurtured those relationships, seeking their guidance and support. Their positive energy and unwavering support have been instrumental in my personal and professional growth.

By disconnecting from negative people and nurturing positive relationships, I have created a social circle that uplifts and empowers me. Surrounding myself with individuals who share my vision, values, and aspirations has propelled me towards success. Evaluating my social circle was a transformative step that allowed me to forge meaningful connections and create a supportive network.

May my testimony inspire you to evaluate your own social circle, discern positive and negative influences, and make intentional choices to disconnect from negativity while nurturing relationships that foster your growth and success.

Chapter 4:

Strategies for Disconnecting

In Chapter 4, we will explore strategies for disconnecting from negative people in order to create a healthier and more positive environment for success. We will delve into building resilience and emotional intelligence, setting healthy boundaries, determining the best approach for disconnecting, communicating our intentions, and coping with the emotional challenges that may arise from this process. These strategies will empower us to take control of our relationships and pave the way for a more fulfilling and successful journey.

Building Resilience and Emotional Intelligence to Deal with Negative People:

Dealing with negative people requires resilience and emotional intelligence. By cultivating these qualities, we can better navigate the challenges and maintain our own well-being.

Scripture provides guidance on building resilience and emotional intelligence:

1. *James 1:2-4:* *"Consider it pure joy, my brothers and sisters, whenever you face trials of many kinds, because you know that the testing of your faith produces perseverance. Let perseverance finish its work so that you may be mature and complete, not lacking anything."* This verse encourages us to find joy in adversity and develop resilience through testing. By embracing the challenges presented by negative people, we can grow in resilience and maturity.

2. *Proverbs 16:32:* *"Better a patient person than a warrior, one with self-control than one who takes a city."* Cultivating emotional intelligence, including self-control and patience, allows us to

respond thoughtfully to negative people rather than reacting impulsively. By developing these qualities, we can maintain our composure and protect our well-being.

Setting Healthy Boundaries and Asserting Yourself in Toxic Relationships:

In toxic relationships, setting healthy boundaries is crucial for our well-being and success. It allows us to protect ourselves from the negative influence of others and create an environment that supports our growth.

Scripture offers guidance on setting boundaries and asserting oneself:

1. **Proverbs 25:28:** *"Like a city whose walls are broken through is a person who lacks self-control."* Setting boundaries is akin to building strong walls around our emotional well-being. It enables us to protect ourselves from the negative impact of toxic

individuals. By establishing clear boundaries and asserting ourselves, we can create a safe space that nurtures our success.

2. *Ephesians 4:15:* *"Instead, speaking the truth in love, we will grow to become in every respect the mature body of him who is the head, that is, Christ."* Asserting ourselves in toxic relationships should be done with love and respect. By speaking our truth kindly and assertively, we can set boundaries while maintaining healthy relationships.

Gradual Distancing versus Abrupt Disconnection: Pros and Cons:

When disconnecting from negative people, we may choose between a gradual distancing approach or an abrupt disconnection. Both have their advantages and considerations, and the choice depends on the specific circumstances.

Scripture encourages wisdom and discernment in our actions:

1. **Proverbs 19:11:** *"A person's wisdom yields patience; it is to one's glory to overlook an offense."* Gradual distancing allows for patience and observation. It provides an opportunity to assess the situation, observe changes in behavior, and make an informed decision about the future of the relationship.

2. **Proverbs 22:10:** *"Drive out the mocker, and out goes strife; quarrels and insults are ended."* Abrupt disconnection may be necessary in cases of extreme toxicity or abusive behavior. It can bring immediate relief from ongoing strife and protect our well-being. However, careful consideration should be given to safety and potential consequences.

Communicating Your Intentions and Reasons for Disconnecting:

When disconnecting from negative people, clear and compassionate communication can help maintain mutual respect and understanding.

Expressing our intentions and reasons for disconnecting can provide closure and minimize misunderstandings.

Scripture guides us in communicating with grace and wisdom:

1. **Ephesians 4:29:** *"Do not let any unwholesome talk come out of your mouths, but only what is helpful for building others up according to their needs, that it may benefit those who listen."* When communicating our intentions, it is essential to choose our words wisely and speak with kindness and respect. This allows for a constructive and compassionate dialogue.

2. **Proverbs 15:1:** *"A gentle answer turns away wrath, but a harsh word stirs up anger."* When communicating our decision to disconnect, a gentle and empathetic approach can help diffuse potential conflict and maintain a positive connection, even if the relationship itself must end.

Coping with Guilt and Loneliness that May Arise from Disconnecting:

Disconnecting from negative people can sometimes bring feelings of guilt and loneliness. It is important to address these emotions and develop coping strategies to navigate this transitional period.

Scripture provides comfort and guidance during challenging times:

1. **Psalm 34:17:** *"The righteous cry out, and the LORD hears them; he delivers them from all their troubles."* When we feel guilty or lonely, we can turn to God for comfort and reassurance. His presence and support can provide solace and strength during this transition.

2. **Hebrews 13:5:** *"Keep your lives free from the love of money and be content with what you have, because God has said, 'Never will I leave you; never will I forsake you.'"* The promise of God's constant presence and faithfulness reminds us that

we are never truly alone. We can find contentment and fulfillment in His presence, even when disconnecting from negative relationships.

Personal Testimony:

In my own journey of disconnecting from negative people, setting healthy boundaries and asserting myself was a transformative process. I realized that I had the power and right to protect my well-being and create an environment that fostered my success.

I gradually distanced myself from toxic individuals, observing changes in their behavior and assessing the impact they had on my life. This approach allowed me to make a decision based on careful consideration rather than impulsive reaction. In other cases, where the toxicity was extreme or abusive, I had to make the difficult choice of abrupt disconnection to safeguard my well-being.

Throughout this process, I communicated my intentions and reasons with compassion and clarity. By expressing my decision to disconnect and setting boundaries, I sought to maintain mutual respect and understanding.

Chapter 5:

Cultivating a Positive Environment

In Chapter 5, we will explore the importance of cultivating a positive environment to support our journey towards success. This involves surrounding ourselves with positive and supportive individuals, finding and building a new network of like-minded people, harnessing the power of mentorship and role models, and creating a positive physical and digital environment. By intentionally cultivating a positive environment, we can enhance our motivation, inspiration, and overall well-being, enabling us to achieve greater success.

Surrounding Yourself with Positive and Supportive Individuals:

The people we surround ourselves with have a significant impact on our mindset, motivation, and success. By intentionally seeking out positive and supportive individuals, we can create an environment that fosters growth and achievement.

Scripture provides guidance on the importance of positive companionship:

1. **Proverbs 13:20:** *"Walk with the wise and become wise, for a companion of fools suffers harm."* Surrounding ourselves with wise and positive individuals can inspire us to grow and become wiser ourselves. Positive companionship helps us stay motivated, focused, and determined on our path to success.

2. **Proverbs 27:17:** *"As iron sharpens iron, so one person sharpens another."* Positive and supportive individuals act as catalysts for personal and professional growth. Their influence can sharpen our skills, expand our knowledge, and propel us towards success.

Strategies for Finding and Building a New Network of Like-Minded People:

Finding and building a new network of like-minded people is essential for creating a positive environment. It involves actively seeking individuals who share similar goals, values, and aspirations, and fostering meaningful connections with them.

Scripture encourages seeking wisdom and like-mindedness:

1. ***Proverbs 18:24:*** *"One who has unreliable friends soon comes to ruin, but there is a friend who sticks closer than a brother."* It is essential to build relationships with reliable and like-minded friends who support us on our journey. These individuals offer encouragement, accountability, and shared experiences, enriching our path to success.

2. **Proverbs 27:9:** *"Perfume and incense bring joy to the heart, and the pleasantness of a friend springs from their heartfelt advice."* Building connections with like-minded individuals allows us to benefit from their advice, perspectives, and wisdom. Their presence brings joy and inspires us to persevere in our pursuit of success.

The Power of Mentorship and Role Models in Achieving Success:

Mentorship and having role models can be powerful catalysts for success. By seeking guidance from experienced individuals and learning from their journeys, we can gain insights, avoid pitfalls, and accelerate our own growth.

Scripture emphasizes the value of seeking guidance from the wise:

1. **Proverbs 1:5:** *"Let the wise listen and add to their learning, and let the discerning get guidance."* Seeking guidance from wise mentors

and role models allows us to expand our knowledge, gain insights, and learn from their experiences. Their wisdom and guidance can illuminate our path to success.

2. **Proverbs 27:17:** *"Iron sharpens iron, and one man sharpens another."* Mentors and role models act as guides who sharpen and refine our skills, attitudes, and behaviors. By observing and learning from their example, we can accelerate our own growth and navigate challenges with greater wisdom.

Creating a Positive Physical and Digital Environment to Support Your Goals:

Creating a positive environment extends beyond relationships to encompass our physical and digital surroundings. By intentionally designing a space that supports our goals and aspirations, we can enhance our motivation, focus, and overall well-being.

Scripture reminds us of the importance of intentional living:

1. **Psalm 119:105:** *"Your word is a lamp for my feet, a light on my path."* Surrounding ourselves with positive and uplifting messages, such as scripture or inspirational quotes, can serve as a constant reminder of our purpose and values. This can help us stay focused and motivated on our journey to success.

2. **Philippians 4:8:** *"Finally, brothers and sisters, whatever is true, whatever is noble, whatever is right, whatever is pure, whatever is lovely, whatever is admirable—if anything is excellent or praiseworthy—think about such things."* Creating a positive physical and digital environment involves intentionally filling our spaces with uplifting and positive elements. From decluttering and organizing our physical surroundings to curating our social media feeds and online content, we can ensure that our environment aligns with our goals and aspirations.

Personal Testimony:

In my own journey, I realized the transformative power of cultivating a positive environment. I actively sought out positive and supportive individuals who shared similar goals and values. Building connections with these like-minded individuals created a network of support and inspiration that propelled me forward on my path to success.

Additionally, I sought mentorship from individuals who had achieved the success I aspired to. Their guidance, wisdom, and willingness to share their experiences were invaluable in shaping my own journey. Having role models to look up to and learn from helped me avoid pitfalls, stay motivated, and continuously grow.

Creating a positive physical and digital environment also played a significant role in my success. I organized my physical space to create a conducive environment for productivity and inspiration. I surrounded myself with uplifting messages, motivational quotes, and reminders of my goals. In the digital realm, I carefully curated my social media feeds, following accounts that provided valuable content and motivation.

By intentionally cultivating a positive environment, I experienced increased motivation, focus, and overall well-being. The support, wisdom, and inspiration from positive individuals and the intentional design of my environment have been instrumental in my success.

May my testimony inspire you to actively seek out positive and supportive individuals, embrace mentorship and role models, and intentionally create a physical and digital environment that nurtures your growth and propels you towards success.

Chapter 6:

Developing a Success Mindset

In Chapter 6, we will explore the importance of developing a success mindset. Cultivating a positive and growth-oriented mindset is crucial for overcoming obstacles, staying motivated, and achieving success. We will delve into strategies for cultivating a success mindset, overcoming negative self-talk and limiting beliefs, staying motivated and focused on our goals, and embracing failures and setbacks as opportunities for growth. By adopting a success mindset, we can unlock our full potential and achieve greater heights of success.

Cultivating a Positive and Growth-Oriented Mindset:

A positive and growth-oriented mindset is the foundation of success. By cultivating this mindset, we can approach challenges with resilience, embrace opportunities for growth, and develop a belief in our ability to achieve our goals.

Scripture provides guidance on cultivating a positive mindset:

1. ***Philippians 4:8:*** *"Finally, brothers and sisters, whatever is true, whatever is noble, whatever is right, whatever is pure, whatever is lovely, whatever is admirable—if anything is excellent or praiseworthy—think about such things."* This verse encourages us to focus our thoughts on positive and uplifting things. By intentionally directing our thoughts towards what is good and praiseworthy, we cultivate a positive mindset that fuels our success.

2. ***Romans 12:2:*** *"Do not conform to the pattern of this world, but be transformed by the renewing of your mind. Then you will be able to test and approve what God's will is—his good, pleasing and perfect will."* Renewing our minds involves consciously changing our thought patterns and beliefs. By aligning our thoughts with God's truth

and focusing on His will for our lives, we transform our mindset and open ourselves to the possibilities of success.

Overcoming Negative Self-Talk and Limiting Beliefs:

Negative self-talk and limiting beliefs can hinder our progress and hold us back from achieving our full potential. Overcoming these internal obstacles is essential for developing a success mindset.

Scripture provides encouragement to overcome negative thinking:

1. **Proverbs 23:7:** *"For as he thinks within himself, so he is."* Our thoughts have a powerful influence on our beliefs and actions. By recognizing and challenging negative self-talk, we can reshape our beliefs and transform our actions. We can replace self-limiting thoughts with empowering affirmations and positive self-talk.

2. **_Philippians 4:13:_** _"I can do all things through Christ who strengthens me."_ This verse reminds us of the strength we have in Christ. By anchoring our beliefs in His power, we can overcome self-doubt and limiting beliefs. We can embrace the truth that we are capable of achieving greatness and pursuing our goals.

Strategies for Staying Motivated and Focused on Your Goals:

Staying motivated and focused on our goals is essential for achieving success. By implementing strategies to maintain our motivation and focus, we can overcome distractions and obstacles along the way.

Scripture offers guidance on staying motivated and focused:

1. **_Proverbs 16:3:_** _"Commit to the LORD whatever you do, and he will establish your plans."_ Committing our goals and aspirations to the Lord ensures that we remain focused and aligned with His purpose for our lives. By seeking His guidance and strength, we can persevere and stay motivated on our journey.

2. **_Hebrews 12:1:_** _"Therefore, since we are surrounded by such a great cloud of witnesses, let us throw off everything that hinders and the sin that so easily entangles. And let us run with perseverance the race marked out for us."_ This verse reminds us to eliminate distractions and obstacles that hinder our progress. By staying focused on the race marked out for us, we can maintain our motivation and endurance.

Embracing Failures and Setbacks as Learning Opportunities:

Failures and setbacks are inevitable on the path to success. Embracing them as learning opportunities allows us to grow, adapt, and ultimately achieve greater success.

Scripture provides wisdom on embracing failures and setbacks:

1. **Romans 8:28:** *"And we know that in all things God works for the good of those who love him, who have been called according to his purpose."* Even in our failures and setbacks, God can work for our good. By viewing these experiences as opportunities for growth and trusting in God's plan, we can persevere and find valuable lessons along the way.

2. **Proverbs 24:16:** *"For though the righteous fall seven times, they rise again, but the wicked stumble when calamity strikes."* The righteous are not immune to failures or setbacks. However, they rise again, learning from their experiences and growing stronger. By adopting a growth mindset, we can see failures as stepping stones to success, rather than roadblocks.

Personal Testimony:

In my own journey, developing a success mindset has been transformative. I realized that the way I approached challenges and setbacks greatly influenced my ability to achieve my goals. By consciously cultivating a positive and growth-oriented mindset, I shifted my perspective and beliefs about myself and my abilities.

I actively worked on overcoming negative self-talk and limiting beliefs by replacing them with affirming and empowering thoughts. I surrounded myself with positive influences, such as inspiring books and podcasts, that reinforced a success mindset. Through prayer and meditation, I sought guidance and strength from God, trusting in His plan for my life.

Staying motivated and focused on my goals required discipline and strategic planning. I set clear objectives, broke them down into smaller milestones, and celebrated each achievement along the way. I also embraced failures and setbacks as opportunities for learning and growth. I analyzed the lessons they offered, adjusted my strategies, and persevered with renewed determination.

By developing a success mindset, I have achieved goals that once seemed unattainable. The transformation in my mindset allowed me to overcome obstacles, stay motivated, and embrace failures as stepping stones to success.

May my testimony inspire you to cultivate a positive and growth-oriented mindset, overcome negative self-talk and limiting beliefs, stay motivated and focused on your goals, and embrace failures as opportunities for growth on your own journey to success.

Chapter 7:

Sustaining Your Success

In Chapter 7, we will explore strategies for sustaining your success by maintaining your disconnection from negative people in the long term. We will discuss strategies for dealing with potential relapses and encountering negativity, building a support system of positive individuals, and engaging in continuous self-reflection and personal development. These practices will help you stay on track, overcome challenges, and continue thriving on your journey towards long-term success.

Maintaining Your Disconnection from Negative People in the Long Term:

Maintaining your disconnection from negative people is crucial for sustaining your success. It requires ongoing commitment and diligence to ensure that you are surrounded by positive influences that uplift and support your growth.

Scripture provides guidance on the importance of staying away from negative influences:

1. *1 Corinthians 15:33:* "Do not be misled: 'Bad company corrupts good character.'" This verse reminds us of the corrupting influence of negative company. To sustain our success, we must continue to distance ourselves from those who bring negativity and hinder our progress.

2. *Psalm 1:1-2:* "Blessed is the one who does not walk in step with the wicked or stand in the way that sinners take or sit in the company of mockers, but whose delight is in the law of the LORD, and who meditates on his law day and night." This passage emphasizes the importance of avoiding the company of those who mock or engage in wrongdoing. By delighting in God's teachings and distancing ourselves from negative influences, we position ourselves for sustained success.

Strategies for Dealing with Potential Relapses and Encountering Negativity:

Despite our best efforts, there may be times when we encounter negativity or face the temptation to reconnect with negative people. Developing strategies to deal with potential relapses is essential for maintaining our progress and staying focused on our goals.

Scripture provides guidance on overcoming temptations and staying steadfast:

1. *James 4:7:* *"Submit yourselves, then, to God. Resist the devil, and he will flee from you."* Submitting ourselves to God's guidance and strength empowers us to resist temptations and overcome relapses. By staying connected to God and seeking His help, we can navigate challenges and maintain our disconnection from negativity.

2. *1 Peter 5:8:* "*Be alert and of sober mind. Your enemy the devil prowls around like a roaring lion looking for someone to devour.*" Staying vigilant and aware of the potential pitfalls and temptations allows us to proactively protect ourselves. By recognizing the tactics of negativity and remaining steadfast, we can sustain our success.

Building a Support System of Positive Individuals Who Encourage Your Success:

Building a support system of positive individuals is vital for sustaining your success. Surrounding yourself with like-minded people who encourage and support your growth can provide ongoing motivation and accountability.

Scripture emphasizes the value of supportive relationships:

1. **Ecclesiastes 4:9-10:** *"Two are better than one because they have a good return for their labor: If either of them falls down, one can help the other up. But pity anyone who falls and has no one to help them up."* Having a support system allows us to lean on others in times of need and receive encouragement and assistance when facing challenges. Together, we can sustain our success and overcome obstacles.

2. **Proverbs 27:17:** *"As iron sharpens iron, so one person sharpens another."* Positive individuals sharpen and inspire us on our journey. By surrounding ourselves with individuals who share our values and aspirations, we can sustain our growth and achieve long-term success.

Continuous Self-Reflection and Personal Development to Sustain Success:

Engaging in continuous self-reflection and personal development is essential for sustaining success. Regularly evaluating our progress, seeking self-improvement, and aligning our actions with our goals keeps us on track and allows for continuous growth.

Scripture encourages self-reflection and personal growth:

1. *Psalm 139:23-24:* *"Search me, God, and know my heart; test me and know my anxious thoughts. See if there is any offensive way in me, and lead me in the way everlasting."* Engaging in self-reflection and inviting God to examine our hearts allows us to identify areas for improvement and realign our actions with our goals. By continuously seeking personal growth, we can sustain our success.

2. *Proverbs 19:20:* *"Listen to advice and accept discipline, and at the end you will be counted among the wise."* Embracing opportunities for learning, receiving feedback, and seeking guidance enables us to continually grow and evolve. By committing to personal development, we sustain our success and reach new heights.

Personal Testimony:

In my own journey, sustaining my success required ongoing commitment to maintain my disconnection from negative people. There were moments when I faced temptations to revisit toxic relationships or encountered negativity in various forms. However, I recognized the importance of staying true to my goals and surrounded myself with positive individuals who encouraged and supported my growth.

When faced with potential relapses, I turned to God for guidance and strength. Through prayer and seeking His wisdom, I found the resilience to resist temptations and stay steadfast on my path. I also built a support system of like-minded individuals who shared my vision and aspirations. Their encouragement and accountability provided ongoing motivation and support, helping me sustain my success.

Continuous self-reflection and personal development were instrumental in my journey.

Regularly evaluating my progress, identifying areas for improvement, and seeking opportunities for growth allowed me to stay focused and aligned with my goals. By listening to advice, accepting discipline, and remaining open to learning, I sustained my success and continued to evolve as an individual.

May my testimony inspire you to stay committed to maintaining your disconnection from negative people, develop strategies to overcome potential relapses, build a support system of positive individuals, and engage in continuous self-reflection and personal development. By implementing these practices, you can sustain your success and achieve long-term fulfillment and growth.

Chapter 8. Conclusion

Recap of the importance of disconnecting from negative people for success:

Throughout this book, we have explored the profound impact that negative people can have on our lives and the crucial role of disconnecting from them in our pursuit of success. We have examined the characteristics and behaviors of negative individuals, the psychological effects of their influence, and strategies for evaluating and reshaping our social circles. Now, as we conclude our journey, let us recap the importance of disconnecting from negative people and the transformation it can bring.

The Scriptures remind us of the significance of surrounding ourselves with positive influences:

1. **Proverbs 13:20:** *"Walk with the wise and become wise, for a companion of fools suffers harm."* This verse emphasizes the power of association, highlighting the importance of choosing our companions wisely. When we surround ourselves with positive and wise individuals, we are more likely to grow and achieve success. Disconnecting from negative people allows us to walk the path of wisdom and avoid unnecessary harm.

2. **1 Corinthians 15:33:** *"Do not be misled: 'Bad company corrupts good character.'"* The company we keep has a direct impact on our character and behavior. Associating with negative people can gradually erode our values, aspirations, and success. By disconnecting from them, we safeguard our character and preserve our journey towards success.

Final thoughts on the journey to success and the role of positive relationships:

As we reflect on our journey to success, it becomes evident that the path is not solely defined by our individual efforts. Positive relationships play a vital role in supporting and nurturing our growth. These relationships uplift us, inspire us, and provide the encouragement we need to overcome obstacles and reach our full potential. Whether it's through mentorship, friendships, or partnerships, positive relationships strengthen us and amplify our chances of success.

The Scriptures offer guidance on the significance of positive relationships:

1. **Proverbs 27:17:** *"As iron sharpens iron, so one person sharpens another."* Just as iron sharpens iron, positive relationships sharpen and refine us. When we surround ourselves with individuals who believe in our potential, challenge us to grow, and provide constructive support, we are propelled forward on our journey to success.

2. **Ecclesiastes 4:9-10:** *"Two are better than one because they have a good return for their labor: If either of them falls down, one can help the other*

up." Success is not meant to be pursued in isolation. Positive relationships provide a safety net, offering support and assistance during challenging times. Together, we can overcome obstacles and accomplish more than we ever could alone.

Encouragement to take action and make positive changes in your social circle:

Now that you have gained a deeper understanding of the impact of negative people and the importance of positive relationships, it is time to take action. The decision to disconnect from negative individuals is not always easy, but it is a vital step toward creating a conducive environment for success. Here are some final thoughts and encouragement to guide you on this transformative journey:

1. ***Proverbs 4:23:*** *"Above all else, guard your heart, for everything you do flows from it."* Your heart and well-being deserve protection. Surround yourself with individuals who uplift and support

you, and distance yourself from those who drain your energy and hinder your progress. Make the conscious choice to prioritize your success by cultivating positive relationships.

2. ***Philippians 4:8:*** *"Finally, brothers and sisters, whatever is true, whatever is noble, whatever is right, whatever is pure, whatever is lovely, whatever is admirable—if anything is excellent or praiseworthy—think about such things."* This verse reminds us to focus our thoughts on positivity and excellence. By disconnecting from negative people, we create space in our lives for thoughts and influences that align with our values and aspirations.

3. ***James 4:8:*** *"Draw near to God, and he will draw near to you."* Disconnecting from negative people also involves drawing closer to God and seeking His guidance. Through prayer, meditation, and seeking wisdom in His Word, we can find strength, clarity, and discernment to navigate the path to success.

In conclusion, success comes when we disconnect from negative people and cultivate positive relationships. By implementing the strategies and insights shared in this book, you have the opportunity to transform your social circle, nurture healthy connections, and create an environment that supports your growth and success. Remember, it is within your power to make positive changes, embrace the journey, and flourish in all aspects of life.

May you embark on this transformative path with courage, determination, and unwavering faith, knowing that success awaits those who choose to disconnect from negativity and surround themselves with positivity.

Best wishes on your journey to success!

[Prophet PD John]